©2017
Book Life
King's Lynn
Norfolk PE30 4LS

ISBN: 978-1-78637-096-9

Written by:
Charlie Ogden

Edited by:
Grace Jones

Designed by:
Danielle Jones

Photo credits

CONTENTS

Words that are <u>underlined</u> are explained in the glossary on page 31.

THE ANIMAL KINGDOM

The animal kingdom includes over 8 million known living <u>species</u>. They come in many different shapes and sizes, they each do weird and wonderful things and they live all over planet Earth.

From the freezing Arctic waters to the hottest desert in the world, animals have <u>adapted</u> to the often extreme and diverse conditions upon Earth.

Even though each and every species of animal is <u>unique</u>, they still share certain characteristics with each other. These shared characteristics are used to classify animals. There are six main groups used to classify animals. They are; mammals, reptiles, birds, insects, amphibians and fish.

10,000 **new** species of animal are discovered **every year.**

Mammals include humans, bears, whales and elephants.

MAMMALS

WHAT IS A MAMMAL?

A mammal is a type of animal that breathes air using lungs, has a backbone and usually grows fur on its body.

Most mammals give birth to live young and produce milk to feed their young. Mammals are warm-blooded animals, which means that they maintain a stable body temperature, even if they live in a very hot or very cold <u>habitat</u>.

Polar bears maintain a stable body temperature even when the temperature outside is below freezing as they are warm-blooded animals.

There are around 5,000 known species of mammal alive today. They come in many different shapes and sizes and they each have their own individual features that help them to survive in their habitats. Humans, lions, elephants and dolphins are all types of mammal.

Blue Whale

Etruscan Shrew

The largest mammal on Earth is the blue whale, which is around 30 metres long. The Etruscan shrew is the smallest mammal on Earth, measuring in at just 4 centimetres long.

MAMMAL CHECKLIST

- 🐾 Give birth to live young
- 🐾 Produce milk to feed their young
- 🐾 Mostly have fur on their bodies
- 🐾 Warm-blooded
- 🐾 Breathe air using their lungs
- 🐾 <u>Vertebrate</u>

BODY PARTS

Mammals come in a lot of different shapes and sizes, which can make it a little difficult to work out whether an animal is a mammal or not! However, there are a few <u>traits</u> that all mammals share with one another.

This does not mean that every mammal has to have every one of these traits – science can't always be perfect! Instead, it means that if an animal has most or all of these traits, then it is probably a mammal.

Mammals are warm-blooded, meaning that they have to keep their bodies at a stable temperature. Many mammals use their fur to keep their body temperatures stable in cold <u>climates</u>.

8

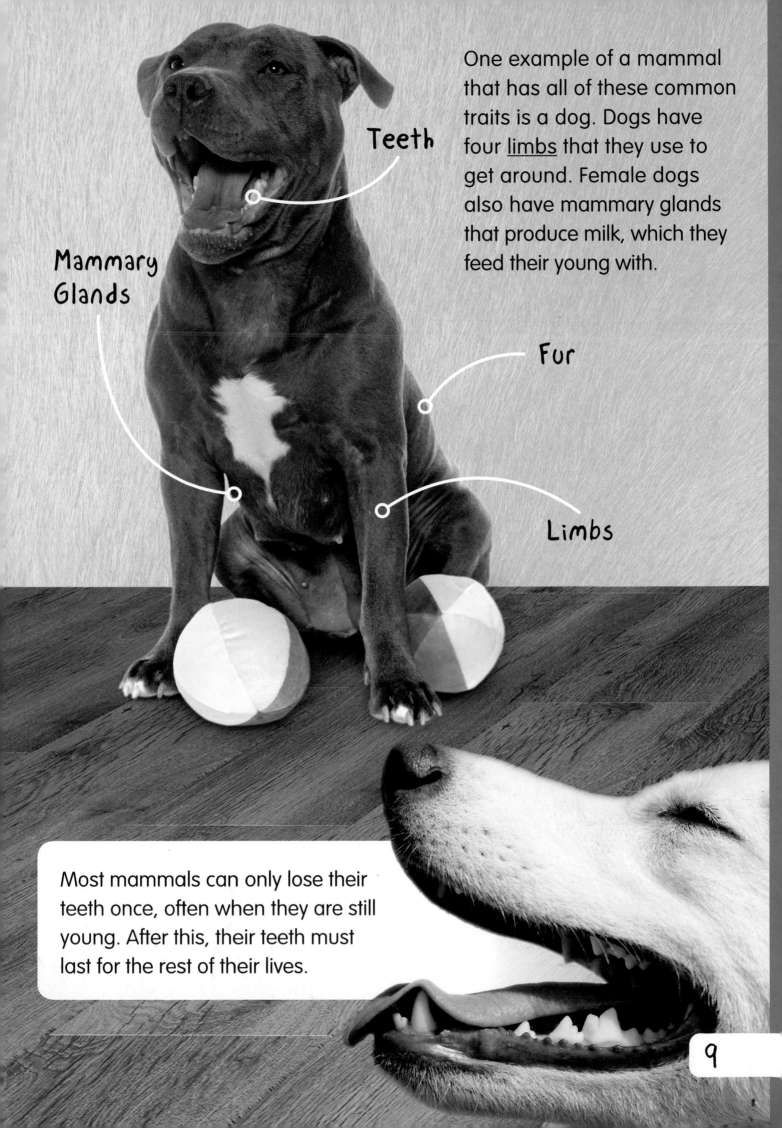

Teeth

Mammary Glands

Fur

Limbs

One example of a mammal that has all of these common traits is a dog. Dogs have four <u>limbs</u> that they use to get around. Female dogs also have mammary glands that produce milk, which they feed their young with.

Most mammals can only lose their teeth once, often when they are still young. After this, their teeth must last for the rest of their lives.

9

ODD ONES OUT

Some animals do not have all of these common traits, but are still classified as mammals.

Dolphins are mammals even though they don't have four limbs or fur! One reason that they are still mammals is because they can't breathe underwater like fish, instead they need to come to the surface to breathe air through their <u>blowholes</u>.

Blowhole

Some **dolphins** can hold their breath for up to **30 minutes!**

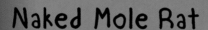

Naked Mole Rat

Naked mole rats are mammals even though they don't have any fur. They are still warm-blooded and they control their body temperature by digging into cold ground when they are hot and cuddling together when they are cold.

Koala

Some traits are only found in a few mammals and not in any other <u>class</u> of animal. One of these traits is a pouch on the stomach where females can keep their young. Mammals that have this pouch are called marsupials and they are mostly found in Australia. A marsupial baby is very weak when it is born, so the mother must keep it in her pouch and feed it milk until it gets stronger. Kangaroos and koalas are both marsupials.

Kangaroos move by jumping forwards with both feet at once. This means that kangaroos can't walk backwards!

11

GETTING AROUND

Mammals move in different ways depending on their habitat. Mammals that only live in trees, like monkeys, koalas and sloths, are known as arboreal mammals. These mammals use their bodies in amazing ways to move through the trees.

Sloth

A group of **monkeys** is called a 'troop' or a 'mission'.

Monkeys have long limbs, sharp claws and strong hands, all of which make it easier for them to grip and swing between branches. They also have a prehensile tail, which is a tail that can grip onto things. Monkeys use their prehensile tails for balance and as an extra way to hold on to trees.

BREATHING

All mammals, including humans, breathe using <u>organs</u> called paired lungs. The lungs pull in and push out air with the help of the diaphragm, which is a muscle that sits just under the ribcage. <u>Oxygen</u> in the air enters the body through the mouth and nose, flows through the larynx, fills the lungs and passes into the <u>bloodstream</u>.

Hiccups are caused by the diaphragm moving when it is not supposed to. This is why you quickly breathe in when you hiccup.

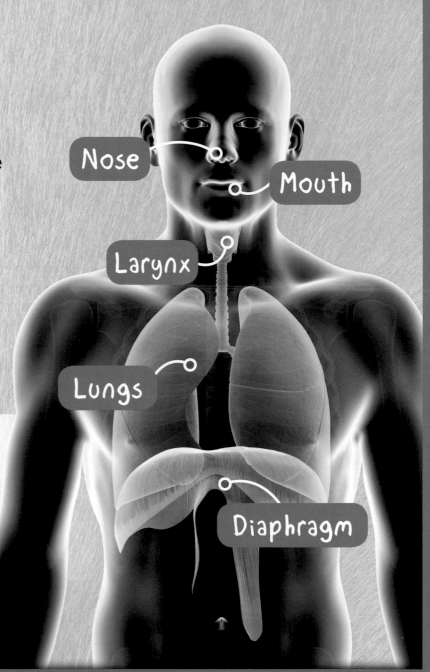

Nose

Mouth

Larynx

Lungs

Diaphragm

PREDATORS AND PREY

All animals can be sorted into groups depending on what they eat. The three groups are carnivores, herbivores and omnivores.

Herbivores
Plant-eaters

Carnivores
Meat-eaters

Omnivores
Plant and meat-eaters

Canine Teeth

Carnivores often have long canine teeth that they use to tear off pieces of meat. The teeth furthest back in the mouth, called molars, will often be flat and <u>blunt</u> in herbivores. These teeth are better for crushing and grinding plants. Omnivores often have both of these types of teeth and they will use their teeth differently depending on what they are eating.

Animals that hunt other animals are called predators, whereas animals that are hunted by other animals are called prey.

It is possible for a mammal to be neither a predator nor prey, like a moose. Moose are herbivores, meaning that they don't hunt other creatures, and they are too big to be the prey of any other animal. It is also possible for a mammal to be both a predator and prey, like the weasel. Weasels eat smaller mammals like mice, rats and rabbits but are often hunted by larger mammals, such as foxes.

LAND, SEA AND 🐾 SKY

Mammals can be found in almost every habitat on land, from jungles and forests to deserts and mountains. However, only a few mammals are able to live in water or in the sky.

Sea otters spend most of their lives floating on their backs in the ocean, using their thick fur to stay warm.

Sea otters are known for using rocks to break open the shellfish that they find. Sea otters and other mammals that live in water are known as aquatic mammals.

Sea otters are one of the only animals on the planet that use tools! Can you think of any others?

Some mammals can also fly through the skies.

Bats have webbed wings that stretch between their limbs and allow them to fly through the forests and caves where they live. Most bats are quite small because it makes it easier for them to fly. However, there are a few species of bat that are so large that they are often called 'megabats' or 'flying foxes'. The golden-capped fruit bat, which lives in forests in the Philippines, is one of the largest bats in the world and can weigh up to 1.2 kg.

Megabat

Bats are the only mammals in the world that can **fly**.

ADAPTATION

Some mammals have adapted to their extreme habitats in many amazing ways in order to survive.

DESERTS

Living in the desert can be dangerous because the high temperatures and the dry climate make it difficult to find water. In desert climates it is easy to become dehydrated, which is when the body doesn't have enough water. If an animal becomes dehydrated, it can die in a matter of hours.

Some desert mammals, like the porcupine, have adapted by becoming <u>nocturnal</u>, meaning that they look for food and water at night when it is cooler.

The long, thick and sharp hairs on a porcupine are called quills and each porcupine has around 30,000 of them.

18

THE ARCTIC

Mammals who live in the Arctic have different problems.

Here there is very little food and temperatures often fall below -40°C. To survive the extreme cold in the Arctic, polar bears have developed smaller ears than other bears, which reduces how much heat they lose.

The polar bear's heavy coat of fur and thick layer of fat also help to keep it warm. When it becomes difficult to find food, a polar bear can use its layer of fat as an emergency store of energy.

Polar bears are the **largest land predators** in the world.

19

LIFE CYCLES

The life cycle of an animal is the series of changes that it goes through from the start to the end of its life.

Possibly the most important part of every life cycle is reproduction, which involves the <u>fertilisation</u> process and the development of young. For nearly all mammals, the fertilisation process occurs inside the female's body and then the female gives birth to live young, instead of laying eggs. The mother will then feed the baby or babies the milk that she produces in her mammary glands.

Elephant mothers will feed their young like this for up to four years.

The platypus has a bill like a duck, a tail like a beaver and feet like an otter!

There are two mammals that lay eggs instead of giving birth to live young, the platypus and the echidna. The way that these mammals reproduce is similar to that of reptiles, which also lay eggs. However, the platypus and the echidna are still mammals as they have mammary glands and they feed milk to their young once they hatch from their eggs. Both of these animals are only found in Australia and on some nearby islands.

The echidna has spines like a porcupine and a nose like an anteater!

LIFE CYCLE OF A ZEBRA

Egg

Zebra mothers hold their babies in the <u>womb</u> for thirteen months, four months longer than human mothers do. This gives the baby more time to grow and means that zebras are able to walk around within an hour of being born.

Adulthood

Zebras go back to living in herds when they are ready to have their own young. Male zebras, called stallions, return to the herd at 3½ years old. Females zebras, called mares, sometimes don't return to their herds until they are 6 years old. Mares can give birth up to six times during their lives.

Foal

Baby zebras, known as foals, will stay very close to their mothers for the first few weeks after they are born. A foal will drink its mother's milk for the first three months of its life.

Colt

After nearly two years, young zebras will leave their <u>herd</u> to live alone or with other young zebras called colts. It is during this time that zebras practise how to find food and water for themselves.

EXTREME MAMMALS

Some mammals have developed extreme habits or skills that help them to survive.

BROWN BEAR

Every autumn, brown bears will start to eat as much food as they can find. This gives the bear a thick layer of fat that it can survive on for the entire winter. In October or November, the brown bear will crawl into a hole or a cave and fall asleep for the next four to seven months. This process is called hibernation.

During hibernation a bear's heartbeat becomes very slow and it can lose up to 40% of its body weight.

Size:
Up to 3 metres long

Home:
Forests and mountains in North America, northern Europe and northern Asia

Diet:
Fruit, roots, bulbs and fish

SOLENODON

Animals that are venomous can protect themselves from other creatures by injecting them with a harmful substance through a bite or a sting. Most venomous animals are reptiles, such as snakes, but some mammals are venomous too! Solenodons have special teeth that can inject venom into their prey or into creatures that are attacking them – just like snakes! Solenodon venom isn't strong enough to kill a person but it would still be extremely painful.

Venomous Fangs

Size:
30 centimetres long

Home:
Hispaniola and Cuba

Diet:
Insects and worms

Solenodons are hard to find because they live underground and are nocturnal. They weren't seen for so long that some people believed that there were none left.

HONEY BADGER

Honey badgers are one of the fiercest animals on the planet.

Honey badgers prey on venomous snakes and scorpions and they are often bitten or stung while they are hunting. This would kill most other animals but honey badgers are able to survive the venom. Honey badgers are not scared of anything and have been known to attack much larger animals when they feel threatened – even lions! The honey badger's extremely thick and rubbery skin helps it to avoid serious injury when it attacks.

Size: **75 centimetres long**
Home: **Africa, Iran and India**
Diet: **Honey, eggs, turtles, rodents, snakes**

The skin of a honey badger is so strong that arrows and spears can't hurt it.

WHALES

Bowhead Whale

Whales are some of the most amazing mammals on the planet.

Bowhead whales have the longest lifespan of any animal on the planet and often live to be over 200 years old! They also have the largest mouth of any animal on the planet.

Size: 18 metres long
Home: Arctic waters
Diet: Crustaceans

Humpback whales make the longest migration of any mammal in the world. These whales spend most of their time in cold Arctic waters, but during the winter they swim 5,000 miles to warmer waters. However, individual humpback whales have been known to make journeys nearly twice this length!

Humpback Whale

Size: 16 metres long
Home: Warm, shallow ocean waters
Diet: Krill and small fish

MAMMALS UNDER THREAT

Lots of the mammals that you have seen in this book are in danger of becoming <u>extinct</u>.

One problem facing these animals is <u>global warming</u>, which could cause the habitats of many mammals to disappear, making it difficult for them to survive.

Global warming could cause the ice that polar bears live on to melt and the areas in Africa where zebras graze to become dry and desert-like, making it difficult for these mammals to find food.

Electricity and other types of energy are made by burning fossil fuels, which are substances that take millions of years to form naturally. When we burn these fossil fuels, certain gases are released into the atmosphere that make it difficult for heat to leave the planet. This is what is causing global warming – but you can help to stop it!

By using less electricity and recycling as much as possible, you can help to save lots of animals from becoming extinct.

Try these energy-saving tips:

• Turn off all lights and electrical devices when you're not using them.

• Cycle or walk as much as possible.

• Take all of your paper and plastic waste to a recycling centre.

FIND OUT MORE

BOOKS

Mammals (Living Things & Their Habitats) by Grace Jones

(BookLife, 2016)

Animal Classification (Discover & Learn) by Steffi Cavell-Clarke

(BookLife, 2017)

WEBSITES

WWF
www.wwf.org.uk

On this website you can follow links to information on all sorts of endangered animals and find out what WWF is doing to save mammals all over the world.

BBC NATURE
www.bbc.co.uk/nature/life/mammal

Discover all the different species of mammal and their habitats.

GLOSSARY

adapted	changed over time to suit an environment
bloodstream	the body system that allows blood to move around the body
blowholes	the holes on top of a dolphin's or whale's head that they use to breathe through
blunt	not sharp
class	a group of animals with similar characteristics
climates	the common weather conditions in certain places
crustaceans	a type of animal that lives in water and has a hard outer shell
extinct	a species of animal that is no longer exists
fertilisation	the process of causing an egg to develop into a new living thing
global warming	the slow rise of the Earth's temperature, in part because of the burning of fossil fuels
habitat	the natural home or environment in which a plant or animal lives
herd	a large group of animals that live together
limbs	body parts of an animal or human
migration	the seasonal movement of animals from one area to another
nocturnal	active at night instead of during the day
organs	parts of an animal that have specific, important jobs
oxygen	a gas that all animals need in order to survive
species	a group of very similar animals that are capable of producing young together
traits	qualities or characteristics
unique	unlike anything else
vertebrate	an animal with a backbone
womb	the organ in the body of a female mammal where the young develop

INDEX